CAUTIONARY
VERSES

The Public Library Series

Old Times on the Mississippi
Mark Twain

Selections from the Koran

Cautionary Verses
Hilaire Belloc

Selections from the Talmud

The Autobiography and Selected
Writings of Abraham Lincoln

Hilaire Belloc's
CAUTIONARY
VERSES

Templegate Publishers
Springfield, Illinois

The special contents of this book
© 1997 Templegate Publishers

Templegate Publishers
302 East Adams Street
Springfield, IL 62701
217-522-3353
www.templegate.com

ISBN 0-87243-234-3
Library of Congress Catalog Card
Number: 97-60839

Cover design: David Brodsky
Interior drawings:
Lisa M. Catalano-Bechtel

**This book was manufactured in
the United States of America**

Child! do not throw this book about;
Refrain from the unholy pleasure
Of cutting all the pictures out!
Preserve it as your chiefest treasure.

Child, have you never heard it said
That you are heir to all the ages?
Why, then, your hands were never
made
To tear these beautiful thick pages!

Your little hands were made to take
The better things and leave the worse
ones.
They also may be used to shake
The Massive Paws of Elder Persons.

And when your prayers complete the
day
Darling, your little tiny hands
Were also made, I think, to pray
For men that lose their fairylands.

CONTENTS

CAUTIONARY TALES FOR CHILDREN

THE BAD CHILD'S BOOK OF BEASTS

MORE BEASTS FOR WORSE CHILDREN

MORE PEERS

CAUTIONARY TALES
FOR CHILDREN

DEDICATED
TO
BOBBY, JOHNNY, AND
EDDIE
SOMERSET

INTRODUCTION

Upon being asked by a Reader
whether the verses contained in this
book were true.
And is it True? It is not True.
And if it were it wouldn't do,
For people such as me and you
Who pretty nearly all day long
Are doing something rather wrong.
Because if things were really so,
You would have perished long ago,
And I would not have lived to write
The noble lines that meet your sight.
Nor B.T.B. survived to draw
The nicest things you ever saw.*

H.B.

*But B.T.B. we could not find
And substituted our own kind.

Ed. note

Jim,

*Who ran away from his Nurse, and was
eaten by a Lion.*

There was a Boy whose name was Jim;
His Friends were very good to him.
They gave him Tea, and Cakes, and
Jam,
And slices of delicious Ham,
And Chocolate with pink inside,
And little Tricycles to ride,
And
    read him Stories through and
through,
And even took him to the Zoo —
But there it was the dreadful Fate
Befell him, which I now relate.

You know — at least you ought to
know,
For I have often told you so —
That Children never are allowed
To leave their Nurses in a Crowd;
Now this was Jim's especial Foible,
He ran away when he was able,
And on this inauspicious day
He slipped his hand and ran away!
He hadn't gone a yard when —

Bang!

With open Jaws, a Lion sprang,
And hungrily began to eat
The Boy: beginning at his feet.
Now just imagine how it feels
When first your toes and then your
heels,
And then by gradual degrees,
Your shins and ankles, calves and
knees,
Are slowly eaten, bit by bit.

No wonder Jim detested it!
No wonder that he shouted "Hi!"
The Honest Keeper heard his cry,
Though very fat

                he almost ran
To help the little gentleman.
"Ponto!" he ordered as he came
(For Ponto was the Lion's name),
"Ponto!" he cried,

              with angry Frown.
"Let go, Sir! Down, Sir! Put it down!"
The Lion made a sudden Stop,
He let the Dainty Morsel drop,
And slunk reluctant to his Cage,
Snarling with Disappointed Rage
But when he bent him over Jim,
The Honest Keeper's

                Eyes were dim.
The Lion having reached his Head,
The Miserable Boy was dead!

When Nurse informed his Parents, they
Were more Concerned than I can say:

His Mother, as She dried her eyes,
Said, "Well — it gives me no surprise,
He would not do as he was told!"
His Father, who was self-controlled,
Bade all the children round attend
To James' miserable end,
And always keep a-hold of Nurse
For fear of finding something worse.

Henry King,

Who chewed bits of String, and was early cut off in Dreadful Agonies.

The Chief Defect of Henry King
Was
            chewing little bits of String.
At last he swallowed some which tied
Itself in ugly Knots inside.
Physicians of the Utmost Fame
Were called at once; but when they came
They answered,
            as they took their Fees,
"There is no Cure for this Disease.
Henry will very soon be dead."
His Parents stood about his Bed
Lamenting his Untimely Death,

When Henry, with his Latest Breath,
Cried —
"Oh, my Friends, be warned by me,
That Breakfast, Dinner, Lunch and Tea
Are all the Human Frame requires..."
With that the Wretched Child expires.

Matilda,

Who told Lies, and was Burned to Death.

Matilda told such Dreadful Lies,
It made one Gasp and Stretch one's
Eyes;
Her Aunt, who, from her Earliest
Youth,
Had kept a Strict Regard for Truth,
Attempted to Believe Matilda:
The effort very nearly killed her,
And would have done so, had not She
Discovered this Infirmity.
For once, towards the Close of Day,
Matilda, growing tired of play,
And finding she was left alone,
Went tiptoe

to

the Telephone
And summoned the Immediate Aid
Of London's Noble Fire-Brigade.
Within an hour the Gallant Band
Were pouring in on every hand,
From Putney, Hackney Downs and
Bow,
With Courage high and Hearts a-glow
They galloped, roaring through the
Town,
"Matilda's House is Burning Down!"
Inspired by British Cheers and Loud
Proceeding from the Frenzied Crowd,
They ran their ladders through a score
Of windows on the Ball Room Floor;
And took Peculiar Pains to Souse
The Pictures up and down the House,
Until Matilda's Aunt succeeded
In showing them they were not needed

And even then she had to pay
To get the Men to go away!

    . . . . .

It happened that a few Weeks later
Her Aunt was off to the Theatre
To see that Interesting Play
The Second Mrs. Tanqueray.
She had refused to take her Niece
To hear this Entertaining Piece:
A Deprivation Just and Wise
To Punish her for Telling Lies.
That Night a Fire *did* break out —
You should have heard Matilda Shout!
You should have heard her Scream and
Bawl,
And throw the window up and call
To People passing in the Street —
(The rapidly increasing Heat
Encouraging her to obtain
Their confidence) — but all in vain!
For every time She shouted "Fire!"

They only answered "Little Liar!"
And therefore when her Aunt returned,
Matilda, and the House, were Burned.

Franklin Hyde,

Who caroused in the Dirt and was corrected by His Uncle.

His Uncle came on Franklin Hyde
Carousing in the Dirt.
He Shook him hard from Side to Side
And
Hit him till it Hurt,
Exclaiming, with a Final Thud,
"Take

         that! Abandoned Boy!
For Playing with Disgusting Mud
As though it were a Toy!—"
            MORAL
From Franklin Hyde's adventure, learn
To pass your Leisure Time

In Cleanly Merriment, and turn
From Mud and Ooze and Slime
And every form of Nastiness —
But, on the other Hand,
Children in ordinary Dress
May always play with Sand.

Godolphin Horne,

Who was cursed with the Sin of Pride,
and Became a Boot-Black.

Godolphin Horne was Nobly Born;
He held the Human Race in Scorn,
And lived with all his Sisters where
His father lived, in Berkeley Square.
And oh! the Lad was Deathly Proud!
He never shook your Hand or Bowed,
But merely smirked and nodded

thus:

How perfectly ridiculous!
Alas! That such Affected Tricks
Should flourish in a Child of Six!
(For such was Young Godolphin's
age).

Just then, the Court required a Page,
Whereat

    the Lord High Chamberlain
(The Kindest and the Best of Men),
He went good-naturedly and

           took

A Perfectly Enormous Book
Called *People Qualified to Be
Attendant on His Majesty,*
And murmured, as he scanned the list
(To see that no one should be missed),
"There's

        William Couts has got the
           Flue,

  And Billy Higgs would never do,
And Guy de Vere is far too young,
And...wasn't D'Alton's Father hung?
And as for Alexander Byng! — ...
I think I know the kind of thing,
A Churchman, cleanly, nobly born,
Come

      let us say Godolphin Horne?"
But hardly had he said the word
When Murmurs of Dissent were heard.
The King of Iceland's Eldest Son
Said, "Thank you! I am taking none!"
The Aged Duchess of Athlone
Remarked, in her sub-acid tone,
"I doubt if He is what we need!"
With which the Bishops all agreed;
And even Lady Mary Flood
(*So* Kind, and oh! so *really* good)
Said, "No! He wouldn't do at all,
He'd make us feel a lot too small."
The Chamberlain said,

      "...Well, well, well!
No doubt you're right....One cannot tell!"
He took his Gold and Diamond Pen
And

      Scratched Godolphin out again.
So now Godolphin is the Boy
Who blacks the Boots at the Savoy.

Algernon,

*Who played with a Loaded Gun, and,
on missing his Sister was reprimanded
by his Father.*

Young Algernon, the Doctor's
    Son,
Was

                    playing with a
                    Loaded Gun.
                    He pointed it to-
                    wards his sister,
                    Aimed very care-
                        fully, but
                          Missed her!
His Father, who was stand-
    ing near,
The Loud Explosion chanced to Hear,

And reprimanded Algernon
For playing with a Loaded Gun.

Hildebrand,

Who was frightened by a Passing Motor, and was brought to Reason.

"Oh, Murder! What was that, Papa!"
"My Child,

It was a Motor-Car,
A Most Ingenious Toy!
Designed to Captivate and Charm
Much rather than to rouse Alarm
In any English Boy.
"What would your Great Grandfather who
Was Aide-de-Camp to General Brue,
And lost a leg at

Waterloo,
And

Quatre-Bras and

Ligny too!
And died at Trafalgar! —
What would he have remarked to hear
His Young Descendant shriek with
fear,
Because he happened to be near
            A Harmless Motor-Car!
But do not fret about it! Come!
We'll off to Town
            And purchase some!"

Lord Lundy,

*Who was too Freely Moved to Tears,
and thereby ruined his Political
Career.*

Lord Lundy from his earliest years
Was far too freely moved to Tears.
For instance if his Mother said,
"Lundy! It's time to go to Bed!"
He bellowed like a Little Turk.
Or if
    his father Lord Dunquerque
Said "Hi!" in a Commanding Tone,
"Hi, Lundy! Leave the Cat alone!"
Lord Lundy, letting go its tail,
Would raise so terrible a wail

As moved
His
    Grandpapa
        the
            Duke
To utter the severe rebuke:
"When I, Sir! was a little Boy,
An Animal was not a Toy!"
His father's Elder Sister, who
Was married to a Parvenoo,
Confided to Her Husband, "Drat!
The Miserable, Peevish Brat!
Why don't they drown the Little
Beast?"
Suggestions which, to say the least,
Are not what we expect to hear
From Daughters of an English Peer.
His grandmamma, His Mother's
Mother,
Who had some dignity or other,
The Garter, or no matter what,

I can't remember all the Lot!
Said "Oh! that I were Brisk and Spry
To give him that for which to cry!"
(An empty wish, alas! for she
Was Blind and nearly ninety-three).
The
Dear old Butler

                    thought — but there!
I really neither know or care
For what the Dear Old Butler thought!
In my opinion, Butlers ought
To know their place, and not to play
The Old Retainer night and day
I'm getting tired and so are you,
Let's cut the Poem into two!

        *   *   *   *   *

Lord Lundy

(SECOND CANTO)

It happened to Lord Lundy then,
As happens to so many men:
Towards the age of twenty-six,
They shoved him into politics;
In which profession he commanded
The income that his rank demanded
In turn as Secretary for
India, the Colonies, and War.
But very soon his friends began
To doubt if he were quite the man:
Thus, if a member rose to say
(As members do from day to day),
    "Arising out of that reply...!"

Lord Lundy would begin to cry.
A Hint at harmless little jobs
Would shake him with convulsive sobs.
While as for Revelations, these
Would simply bring him to his knees,
And leave him whimpering like a child.
It drove his Colleagues raving wild!
They let him sink from Post to Post,
From fifteen hundred at the most
To eight, and barely six — and then
To be Curator of Big Ben!...
And finally there came a Threat
To oust him from the Cabinet!
The Duke — his aged grand-sire —
bore
The shame till he could bear no more.
He rallied his declining powers,
Summoned the youth to Brackley
Towers,
And bitterly addressed him thus —
"Sir! you have disappointed us!

We had intended you to be
The next Prime Minister but three:
The stocks were sold; the Press was
squared:
The Middle Class was quite prepared.
But as it is!...My language fails!
Go out and govern New South Wales!''

. . . . .

The Aged Patriot groaned and died:
And gracious! how Lord Lundy cried!

Rebecca,

Who slammed Doors for Fun and
Perished Miserably.

A Trick that everyone abhors
In Little Girls is slamming Doors.
A
                  Wealthy Banker's
                     Little Daughter
   Who lived in Palace Green,
         Bayswater
(By name Rebecca Offendort),
  Was given to this Furious Sport.
She would deliberately go
And Slam the Door like
     Billy-Ho!
  To make
    her

Uncle Jacob start.
She was not really bad at heart,
But only rather rude and wild:
She was an aggravating child....
It happened that a Marble Bust
Of Abraham was standing just
Above the Door this little Lamb
Had carefully prepared to Slam,
And Down it came! It knocked her flat!
It laid her out! She looked
　　　　　like that.

Her funeral Sermon (which was long
And followed by a Sacred Song)
Mentioned her Virtues, it is true,
But dwelt upon her Vices too,
And showed the Dreadful End of One
Who goes and slams the door for Fun.

　　　． ． ． ． ．

The children who were brought to hear
The awful Tale from far and near
Were much impressed,

and inly swore
They never more would slam the Door.
— As often they had done before.

George,

*Who played with a Dangerous Toy, and
suffered a Catastrophe of considerable
Dimensions.*

When George's Grandmamma was told
That George had been as good as Gold,
She Promised in the Afternoon
To buy him an *Immense BALLOON.*
    And

        so she did; but when it came,
It got into the candle flame,
And being of a dangerous sort
Exploded

             with a loud report!
The Lights went out! The Windows
broke!
The Room was filled with reeking

smoke.
And in the darkness shrieks and yells
Were mingled with Electric Bells,
And falling masonry and groans,
And crunching, as of broken bones,
And dreadful shrieks,when, worst of
all,
The House itself began to fall!
It tottered, shuddering to and fro,
Then crashed into the street below —
Which happened to be Savile Row.

. . . . .

When Help arrived, among the Dead
Were

                 Cousin Mary,
                   Little Fred,

   The Footmen

             (both of them)   ,
                  The Groom,
The man that cleaned the Billiard-
Room,

The Chaplain, and
                The Still-Room Maid.
And I am dreadfully afraid
That Monsieur Champignon, the Chef,
Will now be
                permanently deaf —
And both his
Aides
                are much the same;
While George, who was in part to
blame,
Received, you will regret to hear,
A nasty lump
                behind the ear.

MORAL

The moral is that little Boys
Should not be given dangerous Toys.

Charles Augustus Fortescue,

Who always Did what was Right, and so accumulated an Immense Fortune.

The nicest child I ever knew
Was Charles Augustus Fortescue.
He never lost his cap, or tore
His stockings or his pinafore:
　　In eating Bread he made no
Crumbs,
　　　he was extremely fond
　　　　of sums,
To which, however, he pre-
　　ferred
The Parsing of a Latin
　　Word —
He sought,when it was in

        his power,
For information twice an hour,
And as for finding Mutton-Fat
Unappetising, far from that!
He often, at his Father's Board,
Would beg them, of his own accord,
To give him, if they did not mind,
The Greasiest Morsels they could find.
His Later Years did not belie
The Promise of his Infancy.
In Public Life he always tried
To take a judgement Broad and Wide;
In Private, none was more than he
Renowned for quiet courtesy.
He rose at once in his Career,
And long before his Fortieth Year
Had wedded
Fifi,

                    Only Child
Of Bunyan, First Lord Aberfylde.
He thus became immensely Rich,

And built the Splendid Mansion which
Is called

"The Cedars,
Muswell Hill,"

Where he resides in Affluence still,
To show what Everybody might
Become by

SIMPLY DOING RIGHT.

THE BAD CHILD'S
BOOK OF BEASTS

DEDICATED
To
Master EVELYN BELL
Of Oxford

Evelyn Bell,
I love you well.

INTRODUCTION

I CALL you bad, my little child,
    Upon the title page,
Because a manner rude and wild
    Is common at your age.
The Moral of this priceless work
    (If rightly understood)
Will make you — from a little Turk —
    Unnaturally good.
Do not as evil children do,
    Who on the slightest grounds
Will imitate
        the Kangaroo,
With wild unmeaning bounds:
Do not as children badly bred,
    Who eat like little Hogs,
And when they have to go to bed
    Will whine like Puppy Dogs:

Who take their manners from the Ape,
    Their habits from the bear,
Indulge the loud unseemly jape,
    And never brush their hair.
But so control your actions that
    Your friends may all repeat,
'This child is dainty as the Cat,
    And as the Owl discreet.'

The Yak

As a friend to the children
                commend me the Yak.
  You will find it exactly the thing:
It will carry and fetch,
            you can ride on its back,
Or lead it about with a string.
The Tartar who dwells on the plains of
Thibet
  (A desolate region of snow)
Has for centuries made it a nursery pet,
  And surely the Tartar should know!
Then tell your papa where the Yak can
be got,   And if he is awfully rich
He will buy you the creature—
or else

                he will *not*.
(I cannot be positive which.)

The Polar Bear

The Polar Bear is unaware
  Of cold that cuts me through:
For why? He has a coat of hair.
  I wish I had one too!

The Lion

The Lion, the Lion, he dwells in the
waste,
He has a big head and very small waist;
But his shoulders are stark, and his
jaws they are grim,
And a good little child will not play
with him.

The Tiger

The Tiger on the other hand,
                    is kittenish and mild,
He makes a pretty playfellow for any
little child;
And mothers of large families (who
claim to common sense)
Will find a Tiger well repay the trouble
and expense.

The Dromedary

The Dromedary is a cheerful bird:
I cannot say the same about the Kurd.

The Whale

The Whale that wanders round the Pole
    Is not
                  a table fish.
You cannot bake or boil him whole
    Nor serve him in a dish;
But you may cut his blubber up
    And melt it down for oil.
And so replace
                  the colza bean
       (A product of the soil).
These facts should all be noted down
    And ruminated on,
By every boy in Oxford town
    Who wants to be a Don.

The Hippopotamus

I shoot the Hippopotamus
with bullets made of platinum,
Because if I use leaden ones
        his hide is sure to flatten 'em.

The Dodo

The Dodo used
                to walk around,
    And take the sun and air.
The sun yet warms his native ground—
      The Dodo is not there!
The voice which used to squawk and
squeak
    Is now for ever dumb—
Yet may you see his bones and beak
    All in the Mu-se-um.

The Marmozet

The species Man and Marmozet
Are intimately linked;
The Marmozet survives as yet,
But Men are all extinct.

The Camelopard

The Camelopard, it is said
    By travellers (who never lie),
He cannot stretch out straight in bed
    Because he is so high.
The clouds surround his lofty head,
    His hornlets touch the sky.
How shall
    I hunt this quadruped?
        I cannot tell!

                        Not I!

(A picture of how people try
And fail to hit that head so high.)
I'll buy a little parachute
(A common parachute with wings),
I'll fill it full of arrowroot
And other necessary things

And I will slay this fearful brute
With stones and sticks and guns and
slings.

(Overleaf)

(A picture of

                     how people shoot
With comfort from a parachute.)

The Learned Fish

This learned Fish has not sufficient
brains
To go into the water when it rains.

The Elephant

When people call this beast to mind,
　　They marvel more and more
At such a
　　　　　　LITTLE tail behind,
So *LARGE* a trunk before.

The Big Baboon

The Big Baboon is found upon
    The plains of Cariboo:
He goes about
                with nothing on.
(A shocking thing to do).
But if he
    dressed respectably
And let his whiskers grow,
How like this Big Baboon would be
    To Mister So-and-so!

The Rhinoceros

Rhinoceros, your hide looks all un-
done,
You do not take my fancy in the least:
You have a horn where other brutes
have none:
  Rhinoceros, you are an ugly beast.

The Frog

Be kind and tender to the Frog,
    And do not call him names,
As 'Slimy skin,' or 'Polly-wog,'
    Or likewise 'Ugly James,'
Or 'Gap-a-grin,' or 'Toad-gone-
wrong,'
    Or 'Bill Bandy-knees':
The Frog is justly sensitive
    To epithets like these.
No animal will more repay
    A treatment kind and fair;
At least
                so lonely people say
Who keep a frog (and, by the way,
They are extremely rare).

MORE BEASTS FOR WORSE CHILDREN

Dedication
To
Miss ALICE WOLCOTT
BRINLEY,
Of Philadelphia

MORE BEASTS

FOR WORSE CHILDREN

INTRODUCTION

THE parents of the learned child
  (His father and his mother)
Were utterly aghast to note
The facts he would at random quote
On creatures curious, rare and wild;
  And wondering, asked each other;
  "An idle little child like this,
    How is it that he knows,
  What years of close analysis
    Are powerless to disclose?
Our brains are trained, our books are
      big,
    And yet we always fail

To answer why the Guinea-pig
  Is born without a tail.
Or why the Wanderoo* should rant
  In wild, unmeaning rhymes,
Whereas the Indian Elephant
  Will only read *The Times*.
Perhaps he found a way to slip
  Unnoticed to the Zoo,
And gave the Pachyderm a tip,
  Or pumped the Wanderoo.
Or even by an artful plan
  Deceived our watchful eyes,
And interviewed the Pelican,
  Who is extremely wise."
"Oh! no," said he, in humble tone
  With shy but conscious look,
"Such facts I never could have known
  But for this little book."

*Sometimes called the "Lion-tailed or tufted
Baboon of Ceylon."

The Python

A PYTHON I should not advise,—
It needs a doctor for its eyes,
And has the measles yearly.
However, if you feel inclined
To get one (to improve your mind,
And not from fashion merely),
Allow no music near its cage;
And when it flies into a rage
Chastise it, most severely.
I had an aunt in Yucatan
Who bought a Python from a man
    And kept it for a pet.
She died, because she never knew
These simple little rules and few;—
The Snake is living yet.

The Welsh Mutton

The Cambrian Welsh or Mountain
Sheep
    Is of the Ovine race,
His conversation is not deep,
    But then—observe his face!

The Porcupine

What! would you slap the Porcupine?
    Unhappy child—desist!
Alas! that any friend of mine
    Should turn Tupto-philist.*

To strike the meanest and the least
    Of creatures is a sin,
How much more bad to beat a beast
    With prickles on its skin.

  *From τυπτω = I strike; φιλεω = I
love; one that loves to strike. The word is not
found in classical Greek, nor does it occur
among the writers of the Renaissance—nor
anywhere else.

The Scorpion

The Scorpion is as black as soot,
    He dearly loves to bite;
He is a most unpleasant brute
    To find in bed, at night.

The Crocodile

Whatever our faults, we can always engage
That no fancy or fable shall sully our page,
   So take note of what follows, I beg.
This creature so grand and august in its age,
   In its youth is hatched out of an egg.
And oft in some far Coptic town
The Missionary sits him down
   To breakfast by the Nile:
The heart beneath his priestly gown
   Is innocent of guile;
When suddenly the rigid frown
Of Panic is observed to drown
   His customary smile.
Why does he start and leap amain,

And scour the sandy Libyan plain
Like one that wants to catch a train,
Or wrestles with internal pain?
Because he finds his egg contain—
Green, hungry, horrible and plain—
   An Infant Crocodile.

The Vulture

The Vulture eats between his meals,
    And that's the reason why
He very, very rarely feels
    As well as you and I.
His eye is dull, his head is bald,
    His neck is growing thinner.
Oh! what a lesson for us all
    To only eat at dinner!

The Bison

The Bison is vain, and (I write it with
pain)
    The Door-mat you see on his head
Is not, as some learned professors
maintain,
The opulent growth of a genius' brain;
But is sewn on with needle and thread.

The Viper

Yet another great truth I record in my
verse,
That some Vipers are venomous, some
the reverse;
    A fact you may prove if you try,
By procuring two Vipers, and letting
them bite;
With the *first* you are only the worse
for a fright,
But after the *second* you die.

The Llama

The Llama is a wooly sort of fleecy hairy goat,
With an indolent expression and an undulating throat
  Like an unsuccessful literary man.
And I know the place he lives in (or at least—I think I do)
It is Ecuador, Brazil or Chile—possibly Peru;
  You must find it in the Atlas if you can.
The Llama of the Pampasses you never should confound
(In spite of a deceptive similarity of sound)
  With the Lhama who is Lord of Turkestan.

For the former is a beautiful and valu-
able beast,
But the latter is not lovable nor useful
in the least;
And the Ruminant is preferable surely
to the Priest
Who battens on the woful superstitions
of the East,

The Mongol of the Monastery of
Shan.

The Chamois

The Chamois inhabits
Lucerne, where his habits
   (Though why I have not an idea-r)
Give him sudden short spasms
On the brink of deep chasms,
   And he lives in perpetual fear.

The Frozen Mammoth

This Creature, though rare, is still found to the East
Of the Northern Siberian Zone.
It is known to the whole of that primitive group
That the carcass will furnish an excellent soup,
  Though the cooking it offers one drawback at least
      (Of a serious nature I own):
If the skin be *but punctured* before it is boiled,
Your confection is wholly and utterly spoiled.

And hence (on account of the size of
the beast)
    The dainty is nearly unknown.

The Microbe

The Microbe is so very small
You cannot make him out at all,
But many sanguine people hope
To see him through a microscope.
His jointed tongue that lies beneath
A hundred curious rows of teeth;
His seven tufted tails with lots
Of lovely pink and purple spots,
On each of which a pattern stands,
Composed of forty separate bands;
His eyebrows of a tender green;
All these have never yet been seen—
But Scientists, who ought to know,
Assure us that they must be so....
Oh! let us never, never doubt
What nobody is sure about!

MORE PEERS
Verses by
H. BELLOC

Lord Roehampton

During a late election Lord
Roehampton strained a vocal chord
From shouting, very loud and high,
To lots and lots of people why
The Budget in his own opin-
-Ion should not be allowed to win.
He

        sought a Specialist, who said:
"You have a swelling in the head:
Your Larynx is a thought relaxed
And you are greatly over-taxed."
"I am indeed! On every side!"
The Earl (for such he was) replied
In hoarse excitement...."Oh! My
Lord,
You jeopardize your vocal chord!"
Broke in the worthy Specialist,

"Come! Here's the treatment! I insist!
To Bed! to Bed! And do not speak
A single word till Wednesday week,
When I will come and set you free
(If you are cured) and take my fee."
On Wednesday week the Doctor hires
A Brand-new Car with Brand-new
Tyres
And Brand-new Chauffeur all complete
For visiting South Audley Street.

* * * * *

But what is this? No Union Jack
Floats on the Stables at the back!
No Toffs escorting Ladies fair
Perambulate the Gay Parterre.
A 'Scutcheon hanging lozenge-wise
And draped in crape appals his eyes
Upon the mansion's ample door,
To which he wades through

heaps of Straw,*
And which a Butler, drowned in tears,
On opening but confirms his fears:
"Oh! Sir!—Prepare to hear the worst!...
Last night my kind old master burst.
And what is more, I doubt if he
Has left enough to pay your fee.
The Budget—"

With a dreadful oath,
The Specialist,

denouncing both
The Budget *and* the House of Lords,
Buzzed angrily Bayswaterwards.

———

And ever since, as I am told,
Gets it beforehand; and in gold.

*This is the first and only time
That I have used this sort of Rhyme.

Lord Calvin

Lord Calvin thought the Bishops
should not sit
As Peers of Parliament.

                   And *argued* it!
In spite of which, for years, and years,
and years,
They went on sitting with their fellow-
peers.

Lord Henry Chase

What happened to Lord Henry Chase?
He go into a

                Libel Case!
The Daily Howl had said that he—
But could not prove it perfectly
To Judge or Jury's satisfaction:
His Lordship, therefore,

                won the action.
But, as the damages were small,
He gave them to a Hospital.

Lord Heygate

LORD HEYGATE had a troubled face
His furniture was commonplace—
The sort of Peer who well might pass
For someone of the middle class.
I do not think you want to hear
About this unimportant Peer,
So let us leave him to discourse
About LORD EPSOM and his horse.

Lord Epsom

A Horse, Lord Epsom did bestride
With mastery and quiet pride.
He dug his spurs into its hide.
The Horse,

        discerning it was pricked,
Incontinently

           bucked and kicked,
A thing that no one could predict!
Lord Epsom clearly understood
The High-bred creature's nervous
mood,
As only such a horseman could.
Dismounting,

        he was heard to say
That it was kinder to delay
His pleasure to a future day.
He had the Hunter led away.

Lord Finchley

Lord Finchley tried to mend the Electric Light
Himself.
  It struck him dead: and serve him right!
It is the business of the wealthy man
To give employment to the artisan.

Lord Ali-Baba

Lord Ali-Baba was a Turk
Who hated every kind of work,
And would repose for hours at ease
With
        Houris seated on his knees.
A happy life!—Until, one day
Mossoo Alphonse Effendi Bey
(A Younger Turk: the very cream
And essence of the New Régime)
Dispelled this Oriental dream
By granting him a place at Court,
High Coffee-grinder to the Porte,
Unpaid:—
        In which exalted Post
His Lordship yielded up the ghost.

Lord Hippo

Lord Hippo suffered fearful loss
By putting money on a horse
Which he believed, if it were pressed,
Would run far faster than the rest:
For
someone who was in the know
Had confidently told him so.
But
on the morning of the race
It only took

                the *seventh* place!
Picture the Viscount's great surprise!
He scarcely could believe his eyes!
He sought the Individual who
Had laid him odds at 9 to 2,
Suggesting as a useful tip
That they should enter Partnership

And put to joint account the debt
Arising from his foolish bet.
But when the Bookie—oh! my word,
I only wish you could have heard
The way he roared he did not think
And hoped that they might strike him
pink!
Lord Hippo simply turned and ran
From this infuriated man.
Despairing, maddened and distraught
He utterly collapsed and sought
His sire,

        the Earl of Potamus,
And brokenly addressed him thus:
"Dread Sire—to-day—at Ascot—I..."
His genial parent made reply:
"Come! Come! Come! Come! Don't
look so glum!
Trust your Papa and name the sum....
WHAT?
   ...*Fifteen hundred thousand?*...Hum!

However...stiffen up, you wreck;
Boys will be boys—so here's the
cheque!"
Lord Hippo, feeling deeply—well,
More grateful than he cared to tell—
Punted the lot on Little Nell:—
And got a telegram at dinner
To say
    that he had backed the Winner!

Lord Uncle Tom

Lord Uncle Tom was different from
    What other nobles are.
For they are yellow or pink, I think,
But he was black as tar.
He had his father's debonair
    And rather easy pride:
But his complexion and his hair
Were from the mother's side.
He often mingled in debate
    And latterly displayed
Experience of peculiar weight
    Upon the Cocoa-Trade.
But now he speaks no more. The BILL
    Which he could not abide,
It preyed upon his mind until
    He sickened, paled, and died.

Lord Lucky

Lord Lucky, by a curious fluke,
Became a most important duke.
From living in a vile Hotel
A long way east of Camberwell
He rose in less than half an hour
To riches, dignity and power.
It happened in the following way:—
The Real Duke went out one day
To shoot with several people, one
Of whom had never used a gun.
This gentleman (a Mr. Meyer
Of Rabley Abbey, Rutlandshire),
As he was scrambling through the
brake,
Discharged his weapon by mistake,
And plugged about an ounce of lead

Piff-bang into his Grace's Head—
Who naturally fell down dead.
His heir, Lord Ugly, roared, "You
Brute!
Take that to teach you how to shoot!"
Whereat he volleyed left and right;
But being somewhat short of sight,
His right-hand Barrel only got
The second heir, Lord Poddleplot;
The while the left-hand charge (or
choke)
Accounted for another bloke,
Who stood with an astounded air
Bewildered by the whole affair
—And was the third remaining heir.
After the

            Execution (which
Is something rare among the Rich)
Lord Lucky, while of course, he
needed
Some

help to prove his claim,

        succeeded.

—But after his succession, though
All this was over years ago,
He only once indulged the whim
Of asking Meyer to lunch with him.

Lord Canton

The reason that
                 the present Lord Canton
Succeeded lately to his Brother John
Was that his Brother John, the elder son,
Died rather suddenly at forty-one.
The insolence of an Italian guide
Appears to be the reason that he died.

A
MORAL ALPHABET

A

stands for

        Archibald who told no lies,
And got this lovely volume for a prize.
The Upper School had combed and
oiled their hair,
And all the Parents of the Boys were
there.
In words that ring like thunder through
the Hall,
Draw tears from some and loud ap-
plause from all,—
The Pedagogue, with Pardonable Joy,
Bestows the Gift upon the Radiant
Boy:—
"Accept the Noblest Work produced as
yet"
(Says he) "upon the English Alphabet;

"Next term I shall examine you, to find
If you have read it thoroughly. So
mind!"
And while the Boys and Parents
cheered so loud,
That out of doors
         a large and anxious crowd
Had gathered and was blocking up the
street,
The admirable child resumed his seat.

MORAL

Learn from this justly irritating Youth,
To brush your Hair and Teeth and tell
the Truth.

B stands for Bear.

When Bears are seen
Approaching in the
                distance,
Make up your mind at once between
    Retreat and Armed Resistance.
A Gentleman remained to fight—
    With what results for him?
The Bear, with ill-concealed delight,
    Devoured him, Limb by Limb.
Another Person turned and ran;
    He ran extremely hard:
The Bear was faster than the Man,
    And beat him by a yard.
            MORAL
Decisive action in the hour of need
Denotes the Hero, but does not
succeed.

C

stands for Cobra; when the Cobra
bites
An Indian Judge, the Judge spends rest-
less nights.

MORAL

This creature, though disgusting and
appalling,
Conveys no kind of Moral worth recall-
ing.

D

The Dreadful

                      Dinotherium he

Will have to do his best for D.
The early world observed with awe
His back, indented like a saw.
His look was gay, his voice was strong;
His tail was neither short nor long;
His trunk, or elongated nose,
Was not so large as some suppose;
His teeth, as all the world allows,
Were graminivorous, like a cow's.
He therefore should have wished to
pass
Long peaceful nights upon the Grass,
But being mad the brute preferred
To roost in branches, like a bird.*
A creature heavier than a whale,

You see at once, could hardly fail
To suffer badly when he slid.
And tumbled
                (as he always did).
His fossil, therefore, comes to light
All broken up: and serve him right.
             MORAL
If you were born to walk the ground,
Remain there; do not fool around.

*We have good reason to suppose
  He did so, from his claw-like toes.

E

stands for

Egg.

MORAL
The Moral of this verse
Is applicable to the Young. Be terse.

F

for a

   Family taking a walk
 In Arcadia Terrace, no doubt:
The parents indulge in intelligent talk,
 While the children they gambol about.
At quarter-past six they return to their tea,
Of a kind that would hardly be tempting to me,
 Though my appetite passes belief.
There is Jam, Ginger Beer, Buttered Toast, Marmalade,
With a Cold Leg of Mutton and Warm Lemonade,
And a large Pigeon Pie very skillfully

made
    To consist almost wholly of Beef.

MORAL
A Respectable Family taking the air
    Is a subject on which I could dwell;
It contains all the morals that ever there
were,
    And it sets an example as well.

G

stands for Gnu, whose weapons of Defence
Are long, sharp, curling Horns, and Common-sense,
To these he adds a Name so short and strong,
That even Hardy Boers pronounce it wrong.
How often on a bright Autumnal day
The Pious people of Pretoria say,
"Come, let us hunt the —" Then no more is heard
But Sounds of Strong Men struggling with a word.
Meanwhile, the distant Gnu with grateful eyes
Observes his opportunity, and flies.

MORAL

Child, if you have a rummy kind of name,
Remember to be thankful for the same.

H

was a

Horseman who rode to the meet,
And talked of the Pads of the fox as his
"feet" —
An error which furnished subscribers
with grounds
For refusing to make him a Master of
Hounds.
He gave way thereupon to so fearful a
rage,
That he sold up his Stable and went on
the Stage,
And had all the success that a man
could desire
In creating the Part of
"The Old English Squire."

MORAL

In the Learned Professions, a person
should know
The advantage of having two strings to
his bow.

I

the Poor Indian, justly called "The
Poor,"
He has to eat his Dinner off the floor.
MORAL
The Moral these delightful lines afford
Is: "Living cheaply is its own reward."

J

stands for James, who thought it immaterial
To pay his taxes, Local or Imperial.
In vain the Mother wept, the Wife implored,
James only yawned as though a trifle bored.
The Tax Collector called again, but he
Was met with Persiflage and Repartee.
When James was hauled before the learned Judge,
Who lectured him, he loudly whispered, "Fudge!"
The Judge was startled from his usual calm,
He

struck the desk before him with his
palm,
And roared in tones to make the boldest
quail,
"*J stands for James*, IT ALSO STANDS
FOR JAIL."
And therefore, on a dark and dreadful
day,
Policemen came and took him all away.

MORAL

The fate of James is typical, and shows
How little mercy people can expect
Who will not pay their taxes; (saving
those
To which they conscientiously ob-
ject).

K

for the Klondyke, a Country of
Gold,
Where the winters are often exces-
sively cold;
Where the lawn every morning is cov-
ered with rime,
And skating continues for years at a
time.
Do you think that a Climate can con-
quer the grit
Of the Sons of the West? Not a bit! Not
a bit!
When the weather looks nippy, the bold
Pioneers
Put on two pairs of Stockings and cover
their ears,
And roam through the drear Hyperbo-

rean dales
With a vast apparatus of buckets and
Pails;
Or wander through wild Hyperborean
glades
With Hoes, Hammers, Pickaxes, Mat-
tocks and Spades.
There are some who give rise to exu-
berant mirth
By turning up nothing but bushels of
earth,
While those who have little cause ex-
cellent fun
By attempting to pilfer from those who
have none.
At times the reward they will get for
their pains
Is to strike very tempting auriferous
veins;
Or, a shaft being sunk for some miles
in the ground,

Not infrequently nuggets of value are found.
They bring us the gold when their labours are ended,
And we—after thanking them prettily— spend it.

MORAL

Just you work for Humanity, never you mind
If Humanity seems to have left you behind.

L

was a Lady, Advancing in Age,
    Who drove in her carriage and six,
With a Couple of Footmen, a Coachman and Page,
    Who were all of them regular bricks.
If the Coach ran away, or was smashed by a Dray,
    Or got into collisions and blocks,
The Page, with a courtesy rare for his years,
Would leap to the ground with inspiriting cheers,
While the Footman allayed her legitimate fears,
And the Coachman sat tight on his box.

At night as they met round an excellent meal,

They would take it in turn to observe:
"What a Lady indeed!..what a presence to feel!.."

"What a Woman to worship and serve!..."
But, perhaps, the most poignant of all their delights

Was to stand in a rapturous Dream When she spoke to them kindly on Saturday Nights,

And said "They deserved her Esteem."

MORAL

Now observe the Reward of these dutiful lives:

At the end of their Loyal Career They each had a Lodge at the end of the drives,

And she left them a Hundred a
Year.
Remember from this to be properly
vexed
When the newspaper editors say,
That "The type of society shown in the
Text
Is rapidly passing away."

M

was a Millionaire who sat at Table,
   And ate like this—

            as long as he was able;
At half-past twelve the waiters turned
him out:
   He lived impoverished and died of
gout.

MORAL

Disgusting exhibition! Have a care
When, later on you are a Millionaire,
To rise from table feeling you could
still
Take something more, and not be really
ill.

N

stands for Ned, Maria's younger
brother,
Who, walking one way, chose to gaze
the other.
In Blandford Square—a crowded part
of town—
Two people on a tandem knocked him
down:
Whereat
a Motor Car, with warning shout
Ran right on top and turned him inside
out:
The damages that he obtained from
these
Maintained him all his life in cultured
ease.

MORAL

The law protects you. Go your gentle
way:
The Other Man has always got to Pay.

O

stands for Oxford. Hail! salubrious
seat
Of learning! Academical Retreat!
Home of my Middle Age! Malarial
Spot
Which People call Medeeval (though
it's not).
The marshes in the neighbourhood can
vie
With Cambridge, but the town itself is
dry,
And serves to make a kind of Fold or
Pen
Wherein to herd a lot of Learned Men.
Were I to write but half of what they
know,
It would exhaust the space reserved for

"O";
And, as my book must not be over big,
I turn at once to "P," which stands for
Pig.

MORAL

Be taught by this to speak with modera-
tion
Of places where, with decent applica-
tion,
One gets a good, sound, middle-class
education.

P

stands for Pig, as I remarked before,
A second cousin to the Huge Wild
Boar.
But Pigs are civilised, while Huge Wild
Boars
Live savagely, at random, out of doors,
And, in their coarse contempt for
dainty foods,
Subsist on Truffles, which they find in
woods.
Not so the cultivated Pig, who feels
The need of several courses at his
meals,
But wrongly thinks it does not matter
whether

> He takes them one by one
> > or all together.

Hence, Pigs devour, from lack of self-
respect,
What Epicures would certainly eject.

MORAL

Learn from the Pig to take whatever
Fate
Or Elder Persons heap upon your plate.

Q

for Quinine, which children take
With Jam and little bits of cake.

MORAL

How idiotic! Can Quinine
Replace Cold Baths and Sound
Hygiene?

R

      the Reviewer,

            reviewing my book,

At which he had barely intended to look;

But the very first lines upon "A" were enough

To convince him the *Verses* were excellent stuff.

So he wrote, without stopping, for several days

In terms of extreme but well-merited Praise.

To quote but one Passage: "No Person" (says he)

"Will be really content without purchasing three,

"While a Parent will send for a dozen

or more,
And strew them about on the Nursery
Floor.

"The Versification might call for some
strictures

"Were it not for its singular wit; while
the Pictures,

"Tho' the handling of line is a little
defective,

"Make up amply in *verve* what they
lack in

                    perspective."
MORAL
The habit of constantly telling the Truth
Will lend an additional lustre to Youth.

S

stands for Snail, who, though he be the least,

Is not an uninstructive Hornèd Beast.

His eyes are on his Horns, and when you shout

Or tickle them, the Horns go in and out.

Had Providence seen proper to endow

The furious unicorn or sober Cow

With such a gift, the one would never now

Appear so commonplace on Coats of Arms.

And what a fortune for our failing farms

If circus managers, with wealth untold,

Would take the Cows for half their weight

in gold!

MORAL

Learn from the Snail to take reproof
with patience,
And not put out your Horns on all
occasions.

T

for the Genial Tourist, who resides
In Peckham, where he writes Italian
Guides.

MORAL

Learn from this information not to cavil
At slight mistakes in books on foreign
travel.

U

for the Upas Tree,

that casts a blight
On those that pull their sisters' hair,
and fight.
But oh! the Good! They wander undis-
mayed,
And (as the Subtle Artist has portrayed)
Dispend the golden hours at play be-
neath its shade.*

MORAL

Dear Reader, if you chance to catch a
sight
Of Upas Trees, betake yourself to
flight.

*A friend of mine, a Botanist, believes
That Good can even browse upon its leaves.
I doubt it....

V for

the unobtrusive Volunteer,
Who fills the armies of the World with
fear.
MORAL
Seek with the Volunteer to put aside
The empty Pomp of Military Pride

W

My little victim, let me trouble you
    To fix your active mind on W.
The WATERBEETLE here shall teach
A sermon far beyond your reach:
He flabbergasts the Human Race
By gliding on the water's face
With ease, celerity, and grace;
But if he ever stopped to think
Of how he did it, he would sink.
MORAL
Don't ask Questions!

X

No reasonable little Child expects
A Grown-up Man to make a rhyme on
X.
MORAL
These verses teach a clever child to find
Excuse for doing all that he's inclined.

Y

stands for Youth (it would have stood for Yak,
But that I wrote about him two years back).
Youth is the pleasant springtime of our days,
As Dante so mellifluously says
(Who always speaks of Youth with proper praise).
You have not got to Youth, but when you do
You'll find what He and I have said is true.

MORAL

Youth's excellence should teach the Modern Wit
First to be Young, and then to boast of it.

Z

for this Zébu, who (like all Zebús)*
Is held divine by scrupulous Hindoos.

MORAL

Idolatry, as you are aware,
Is highly reprehensible. But there,
We needn't bother—when we get to Z
Our interest in the Alphabet is dead.

*Von Kettner writes it "ZEbu"; Wurst
"ZeBU":
I split the difference and use the two.

LADIES
AND GENTLEMEN

Dedicated to
ELVIRA WALLER TURTON

I
The Garden Party

The Rich arrived in pairs
And also in Rolls Royces;
They talked of their affairs
In loud and strident voices.
(The Husbands and the Wives
Of this select society
Lead independent lives
Of infinite variety.)
The Poor arrived in Fords,
Whose features they resembled,
They laughed to see so many Lords
And Ladies all assembled.
The People in Between
Looked underdone and harassed,
And out of place and mean,
            And horribly embarrassed.

For the hoary social curse
Gets hoarier and hoarier,
And it stinks a trifle worse
   Than in
The days of Queen Victoria,

   when

They married and gave in marriage,
They danced at the County Ball,
And some of them kept a carriage.
AND THE FLOOD DESTROYED THEM
ALL.

II
William Shand

There was a man called WILLIAM
SHAND,
He had the habit of command,
And

       when subordinates would shout
He used to bang them all about.
It happened by a turn of Fate,
Himself became sub-ordinate,
Through being passenger upon
A liner, going to Ceylon
One day, as they were in the Red
(Or Libyan) Sea,

       the Captain said:
"I think it's coming on to blow.
Let everybody go below!"
But William Shand said: "Not for me.

I'm going to stop on deck!'' said he.
The Captain, wounded in his pride,
Summoned the Second Mate aside
And whispered: "Surely Mr. Shand
Must be extremely rich by land?''
"No,'' said the Mate, "when last ashore
I watched him. He is rather poor.''
"Ho!'' cried the Captain. "Stands it thus?
And shall the knave make mock of us?
I'll teach him to respect his betters.
Here Bo'swain! Put the man in fetters!''
In fetters therefore

        William lay
Until the liner

        reached Bombay,
When he was handed to the court
Which deals with cases of the sort

In that uncomfortable port;
Which
promptly
   hanged him
     out of hand.
Such was the fate of William Shand.

MORAL
The moral is that people must,
If they are poor, obey or bust.

III
The Three Races

I

Behold, my child,
        the Nordic Man
And be as like
        him as you can.
His legs are long;
        his mind is slow;
His hair is lank
        and made of tow.

II

And here we have the Alpine Race.
Oh! What a broad and foolish face!
His skin is of a dirty yellow,
He is a most unpleasant fellow.

III

The most degraded of them all
Mediterranean we call.
His hair is crisp, and even curls,
And he is saucy with the girls.

IV
Obiter Dicta

SIR HENRY WAFFLE K.C. (continuing)

Sir Anthony Habberton, Justice and
Knight,
Was enfeoffed of two acres of land
And it doesn't
   sound much
       till you hear that the site
Was a strip to the South of the Strand.
HIS LORDSHIP (Obiter Dictum)
A strip to the South of the Strand
Is a good situation for land.
It is healthy and dry
And sufficiently high
And convenient on every hand.

II

SIR HENRY WAFFLE K.C. *(continuing)*
Now Sir Anthony, shooting in Timber-
ley Wood,
Was imprudent enough to take cold;
And he
died without warning at six in the
morning,
    Because he was awfully old.
HIS LORDSHIP *(Obiter Dictum)*
I have often been credibly told
    That when people are awfully old
    Though cigars are a curse
    And
        strong waters are worse
    There is nothing so fatal as cold.

III

SIR HENRY WAFFLE K.C. *(continuing)*
But Archibald answered on hearing the
news:—
"I never move out till I must."

Which was all very jolly for *Cestui que Use*
But the Devil for *Cestui que Trust*.

HIS LORDSHIP *(ObiterDictum)*
The office of *Cestui que Trust*
Is reserved for the learned and just.
Any villain you *chose*
May be *Cestui que Use,*
But a Lawyer for *Cestui que Trust*.

IV

SIR HENRY WAFFLE K.C. *(continuing)*
Now the ruling laid down
       in *Regina v. Brown*
May be cited....

HIS LORDSHIP *(rising energetically)*
You're wrong!
    It may not!
I've strained all
   my powers
      For some thirty-six hours
       To unravel this pestilent rot.

THE WHOLE COURT *(rising and singing in chorus)*
Your Lordship is sound to the core.
It is nearly a quarter to four.
We've had quite enough
         Of this horrible stuff
And we don't want to hear any more!
LITTLE SILLY MAN *(rising at the back of the Court)*
Your Lordship is perfectly right.
He can't go on rhyming all night.
I suggest...

   (He is gagged, bound and dragged off to a Dungeon.)

180

V
The Statesman

I knew a man who used to say,
Not once but twenty times a day,
   That in
               the turmoil and the strife
  (His very words) of Public Life
    The thing of ultimate effect
Was Character—   not Intellect.
He therefore was at strenuous pains
To atrophy his puny brains
And registered success in this
Beyond the dreams of avarice,
Till, when he had at last become
Blind,
paralytic, deaf and dumb,
Insensible and cretinous,
He was admitted

ONE OF US.

They therefore, (meaning Them by
"They")

His colleagues of the N.C.A.,
The T.U.C.,
the I.L.P.

Appointed him triumphantly
To bleed the taxes of a clear
200,000 Francs a year
(Swiss),

as the necessary man

For

Conferences at Lausanne,
Geneva, Basle, Locarno, Berne:
A salary which he will earn,
Yes—*earn* I say—

until he Pops,

Croaks, passes in his checks and
Stops:—
When he will be remembered for
A week, a month, or even more.

VI
The Author

There is a literary man,
Whose name is
        Herbert Keanes:
His coat is lined with astrachan.
He lives on private means.
   His house is in St. James's Square
       (Which I could not afford).
   His head is strong but short of hair,
          His Uncle is a Lord.
This Uncle loves him
      like a son
And has been heard to vow
He will be famous later on
And even might be now.
And he has left him in his will
New Boyton, Hatton Strand,

Long Stokely, Pilly-on-the-Hill,
And Lower Sandiland.

He is not dead, but when he dies
This wealth will all accrue,
Unless the old gafoozler lies,
O Herbert Keanes, to you!

The Son? The Son whom *She* alone
Could bear to such a sire,
The son of Lady Jane O'Hone
And Henry Keanes Esquire.
First with a private tutor,
    then
At Eton Herbert Keanes,
Like other strong successful men,
Was nurtured in his teens.
To curious dons he next would pay
His trifling entrance fee,
And was accepted, strange to say,
By those of Trinity.

Tall Trinity whereby the Cam
Its awful torrent rolls,
But there!—I do not care a damn,
It might have been All Souls.
Has sat for Putticombe in Kent
But lost the seat he won
By boldly saying what he meant
Though meaning he had none.
Has written "Problems of the Poor,"
    "The Future
    of Japan"
        And "Musings by
        Killarney's Shore"
                And
"What Indeed
    is Man?"
    And
"Flowers and Fruit"
(a book of verse)
                    "The Ethics
                    of

St. Paul,"
"Was there a Peter?"
(rather worse)

And
"Nero"
(worst of all).
Clubs: Handy Dandy, Beagle's,
Tree's,
Pitt, Palmerston, Riviere,
The Walnut Box, Empedocles,
Throgmorton, Pot o' Beer.
(The last for its bohemian lists
Wherein he often meets
Old Wasters,

Poets,
Communists,
And Ladies from the Streets.)
A strong Protectionist, believes
In everything but Heaven.
For entertainment, dines, receives,
Unmarried, 57.

VII
The Example

John Henderson, an unbeliever,
Had lately lost his Joie de Vivre
From reading far too many books.
He went about with gloomy looks;
Despair inhabited his breast
And made the man a perfect pest.
Not so his sister, Mary Lunn,
She had a whacking lot of fun!
Though unbelieving as a beast
She didn't worry in the least.
But drank as hard as she was able
And sang and danced upon the table;
                                    And
     when she met her brother Jack
She used to smack him on the back
So smartly as to make him jump,

And cry, "What-ho! You've got the
hump!"
A phrase which, more than any other,
Was gall and wormwood to her
brother;
For, having an agnostic mind,
He was exceedingly refined.
The Christians, a declining band,
Would point with monitory hand
To Henderson his desperation,
To Mary Lunn her dissipation,
And often mutter, "Mark my words!
Something will happen to those birds!"
Which came to pass: for

                Mary Lunn
Died suddenly, at ninety one,
Of Psittacosis, not before
Becoming an appalling bore.
While Henderson, I'm glad to state,
Though naturally celibate,

Married an intellectual wife
Who made him lead the Higher life
And
          wouldn't give him any wine;
Whereby he fell in a decline,
And, at the time of writing this,
Is suffering from paralysis,
The which, we hear with no surprise,
Will shortly end in his demise.

MORAL

The moral is (it is indeed!)
You mustn't monkey with the Creed.